GEORGE W. BUSH
The Family Business

DANIEL COHEN

A Gateway Biography
The Millbrook Press
Brookfield, Connecticut

Published by The Millbrook Press, Inc.
2 Old New Milford Road
Brookfield, CT 06804
www.millbrookpress.com

Library of Congress Cataloging-in-Publication Data
Cohen, Daniel, 1936–
George W. Bush : the family business / Daniel Cohen.
  p. cm. — (Gateway biography)
Includes bibliographical references and index.
ISBN 0-7613-1851-8 (lib. bdg.) — ISBN 0-7613-1383-4 (pbk.)
1. Bush, George W. (George Walker), 1948– 2. Governors—Texas—Biography.
3. Presidential candidates—United States—Biography. 4. Texas—Politics and
government—1951– . 5. Children of presidents—United States—Biography.
I. Title. II. Series.
F391.4.B87 C64 2000   976.4'063'092—dc21   [B]   99-054082

Text copyright © 2000 by Daniel Cohen

Cover photograph courtesy of Liaison Agency/Lee Celand
Photographs courtesy of Corbis/AFP: pp. 7, 13; George Bush Presidential Library:
pp. 9, 17, 19, 20, 23, 24, 29, 37; Corbis/Bettmann-UPI: p. 26; Liaison Agency: p. 33
(© David Woo); AP/Wide World Photos: pp. 34, 43; Reuters/Gerald Reed
Schumann/Archive Photos: p. 38; Corbis/Reuters Newsmedia, Inc.: p. 41

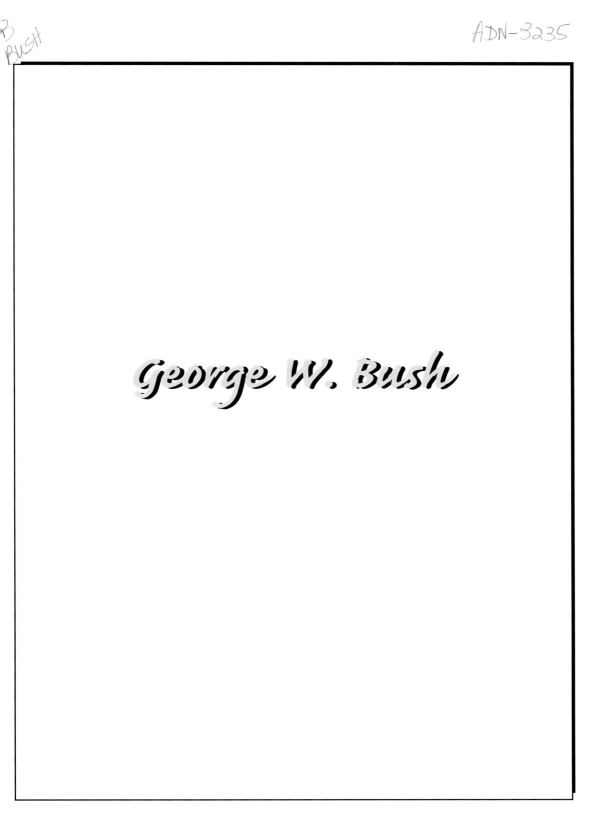

George W. Bush

*I*n America, politics has often been a family business.

John Adams was the second president of the United States. His son John Quincy Adams was the sixth president.

Theodore Roosevelt was the twenty-sixth president. His cousin Franklin Delano Roosevelt was the thirty-second president.

William Howard Taft was the twenty-seventh president. His son Robert Taft was a senator from Ohio. Robert Taft tried, unsuccessfully, to gain the Republican presidential nomination three times.

John Fitzgerald Kennedy was the thirty-fifth president. His brother Robert Kennedy was senator from New York. Their youngest brother, Edward Kennedy, is a senator from Massachusetts. Other members of the large Kennedy family are in the House of Representatives or hold other political offices.

George W. Bush also comes from a political family. His grandfather, Prescott Bush, was a wealthy and successful banker and a Republican senator from Connecticut. George W.'s father, George Herbert Walker Bush, was the forty-first president. George's brother Jeb was elected governor of Florida. George himself was elected Governor of Texas and entered the race for the presidency in 1999.

George W.'s father, George Herbert Walker Bush, was born in Massachusetts in 1924. The family later moved to Connecticut. However, when George was old enough he was sent to boarding school back in Massachusetts, to Phillips Academy in Andover. The school is one of the most exclusive and expensive prep schools in the country.

By the time George Bush graduated, World War II had started. He joined the navy, became a pilot, and flew many dangerous missions in the Pacific. He was shot down once and was a genuine war hero. When the war was over he finished his education at Yale University, in Connecticut.

In 1945 George Bush married Barbara Pierce, the daughter of a publishing executive and banker. The couple had met before the war. A year later, on July 6, 1946 their first son, George Walker Bush, was born in New Haven, Connecticut. His father was still a student at Yale.

When George Bush graduated in 1948 the family moved to Odessa, Texas. George had a job working for an oil drilling equipment company owned by the father of a Yale classmate.

After a year the family was briefly transferred to California, where their daughter, Pauline Robinson (Robin), was born.

A 1948 family portrait of the Bushes, showing from left to right Barbara, George W., George, and his parents Dorothy Walker Bush and Prescott Bush.

By 1950 they were back in Texas, living in the city of Midland. Midland, in West Texas, is the center of the Texas oil country. In 1950 an oil boom was just beginning. George Bush started his own oil company. The company was a success. The family moved from a small apartment to a small house, and eventually to a very large house with a pool. Midland, Texas, is where George W. Bush really grew up.

In February 1953, a second Bush son, John Ellis (Jeb), was born.

A few weeks after Jeb's birth, Robin became ill. Her parents took her to Memorial Sloan Kettering cancer hospital in New York. Tests showed that she had advanced leukemia.

On an October day in 1953 George and Barbara Bush went to pick up their young son at school. They had to tell him that his sister, Robin, had died. The boy was shattered. He knew his sister had been sick but he had no idea she was dying.

Years later George W. would tell some of his friends, "You think your life is so good and everything is perfect; then something like this happens and nothing is the same."

George W. went to Sam Houston Elementary school. Friends remember him as an active youngster—good at sports and usually the center of attention. He was popular and a leader. Sometimes he led his friends on risky adventures, like climbing the light poles around the high school athletic stadium.

With his chaps and a ten-gallon hat, George W. looks right at home on top of this pony.

During most of those early years his mother, Barbara, was the biggest influence on his life. Like most Midland oilmen of the time, George Bush Senior worked long hours and did a lot of traveling. Barbara was in charge of the growing Bush family. Another son, Neil Mallon, was born in 1955 and a fourth, Marvin Pierce, in 1956. Daughter Dorothy Walker was born in 1959.

Barbara Bush has made it clear that her job wasn't always easy. She talks of "diapers, runny noses, earaches, more Little League games than you could believe possible. . ." She also talks of low times when she had the feeling "I'd never have fun again."

In 1958 George W. entered San Jacinto Junior High in Midland. He became quarterback on the school football team and class president. That was his last year in public school.

The following year the Bush family moved to Houston, Texas. George W.'s parents enrolled him in a private school called the Kinkaid School. George W. fit right in. He became a class officer and made the football team. He also had a gift for making friends.

One thing that all his friends remember about him is that he was no snob. He was just the opposite. If someone had a fancy car he would say that it was too fancy for his blood.

Every summer the family would pile into the car and drive cross-country to the Bush family summer home in Kennebunkport, Maine. In 1961 his parents decided that he should continue his education at Phillips Academy in Andover, Massachusetts, where his father had gone to school.

The change to Andover was not an easy one. Fifteen-year-old George W. had never lived away from home before. He also felt he had to live up to his father's reputation. The senior Bush had been an outstanding student, president of his class, and captain of the baseball team. George W. was a very average student. While he played a lot of sports, he was never a star. Instead he became a cheerleader for the varsity football team. But he was fun to be with and he made a lot of friends. The other students noticed him. He was nicknamed "Lip" because he had an opinion about everything.

In his senior year at Andover, George W. applied to two colleges. One was the University of Texas, the other was Yale University, where his father had gone. His grandfather and some of his uncles were also Yale men. George W. didn't think his Andover grades were good enough to get him into Yale. He was surprised when he was accepted.

George W. arrived at Yale in the fall of 1964. At the same time his father began his career in the real Bush family business, politics. As always, Bush Senior discussed his decision with his family. They all approved. He became the Republican candidate for senator from Texas. The year 1964 was not a good time to run as a

Republican, particularly in Texas. The Democratic party candidate for president was Texan Lyndon B. Johnson. Johnson won in a landslide. George Bush Senior was defeated by 300,000 votes.

At Yale George W. joined the Delta Kappa Epsilon fraternity. In his senior year he was elected fraternity president. He played a variety of sports. He majored in history, but by all accounts he was only a fair student. All in all, he does not seem to have enjoyed his time at Yale very much. He said the university had too many "intellectual snobs."

There was another reason for feeling uncomfortable at Yale. While George W. was at Yale the war in Vietnam was raging. He was in favor of the United States' role in the war. Most Yale students were against it.

Back in Texas, Bush Senior was becoming more involved in politics. Even though he had been defeated in his run for the U.S. Senate, he decided to go into politics full time. He sold his oil company and ran for the U.S. House of Representatives from the Houston area. This time he won. He was becoming well known to Republicans, not only in Texas but throughout the country.

On May 27, 1968, two weeks before he was to graduate from Yale, George W. Bush went to the offices of the Texas Air National Guard and signed up. He barely passed a "pilot aptitude" test. There usually was a long waiting list to get into the Air National Guard. George W. was accepted immediately. Officials of the Guard say

George Bush, then a Congressman from Houston, Texas, pins bars on George W.'s uniform, to mark his entry as 2nd Lieutenant in the Texas Air National Guard.

that he was not given special treatment. But they certainly knew his father was a congressman who supported the war. The sons of many other influential people managed to avoid being drafted by getting into the National Guard.

Once George W. graduated he almost certainly would have been drafted into the army. The war in Vietnam was at its height. There is a good chance that he would have been sent into battle. In the Air National Guard there was almost no chance that he would be sent to Vietnam.

George W. insists that he was not trying to avoid fighting. He says he wanted to be an Air Force pilot like his father. If he had been ordered to go to Vietnam he would have gone.

He was required to spend two years in flight training and another four years in part-time service. After he finished his basic training he received the rank of second lieutenant. In 1968 George W. was able to take a two-month vacation to work for a Republican candidate for the Senate in Florida.

George Bush Senior's political career was advancing quickly. He ran for the Senate again, and lost again. But he was then appointed Chairman of the Republican National Committee. That was an important political job and a big step up.

In flight school George W. became an excellent pilot. He never boasted about his family's political connections. He barely ever talked about them. But something happened that made him famous among the other trainees. In the middle of his training, President Richard M. Nixon sent a special plane to take him on a date with his daughter, Tricia. There never was a second date, but nobody at the Air Base ever forgot the story.

After he graduated from Combat Crew Training School in June 1970, he had four more years of part-time military duty. George W. Bush didn't seem to know what he was going to do so he took a series of different jobs.

Some of the time he worked as a counselor in a program for African-American youths in Houston. He was very popular. One of his co-workers remembers him this way:

"He had a bomb of a car. It was the pits . . . always full of stuff, like clothes and papers. No one could ride in it with him. . . . He never put himself in the position of looking down his nose at someone, like, 'I've got all this money, my father is George Bush.' He never talked about his father. He was so down to earth. . . . You could not help liking him. He was always fun."

As his commitment to the Air National Guard came near its end, George W. applied to the University of Texas law school. He was rejected. He also applied to Harvard University Business School. There he was accepted.

At Harvard Business School, George W. stood out. The school was filled with people who expected to make a career in big business. Students were usually well groomed and well dressed. Bush arrived at Harvard in Cambridge, Massachusetts, in his beat-up old car. He wore scruffy clothes. One picture of him in the yearbook shows him sitting in the back of a class blowing bubble gum. It was not what people expected from the twenty-seven-year-old son of the Republican National Committee chairman.

George W. did not look like a man who was planning a career on Wall Street. Everyone assumed that after he graduated from Harvard he would go right back to Texas.

After earning a masters degree in business administration (MBA), George W. headed west. He said he was going to visit a buddy's ranch in Tucson, Arizona. Along the way he stopped to visit old friends in Midland, Texas, where he had grown up. Many of his old friends were going into the oil business. His father had been in the oil business. So George W. decided to try his hand at it.

He was too restless and impatient to work for an established oil company. He started out as a freelance land man. He spent his days in county courthouses looking up mineral rights and trying to make deals to lease them.

That wasn't enough for the energetic and impulsive young man. In 1977 he decided to run for congress. He had already worked on three of his father's campaigns. He had been on the staff of two other Republican senate candidates. A long-time Democratic congressman from

*Early days on the campaign trail
with his wife-to-be, Laura.*

the area was retiring. Republicans thought they had a good chance to pick up the seat. George W. jumped into the Republican primary late. He had a familiar name and was a good campaigner. He won the primary.

George W.'s decision to run for office did not surprise his friends. His decision to get married did. He had a reputation for being a bit wild, not at all the sort of person who was ready to settle down.

Ten days after he became a candidate he met Laura Welch at a cookout in Midland. She was a thirty-year-old librarian who had grown up in Midland. She was as quiet as Bush was loud. They were a most unlikely couple. Three months later, on November 5, 1977, they were married.

The couple's twin daughters, Barbara and Jenna, were born in 1981.

George W. had promised his wife that she would never have to make a campaign speech. "We campaigned the whole first year of our marriage," Laura told *Time* magazine.

George W. was a good campaigner. His opponent, State Senator Kent Hance, was better. Hance had been born in Texas and spent his whole life in Texas politics. He managed to make George W. look like an outsider.

Hance said that his "daddy and grandad were farmers." He pointed out that he had gone to school in Texas while Bush was educated at Andover, Yale, and Harvard. On it went. Hance won the election easily. George W. Bush learned some hard lessons about poli-

George W. with his newborn twins.

tics. Most importantly, he learned that you have to be from somewhere. It helps to have a "hometown" rooting for you. Today George stresses his Texas upbringing.

After the tough election campaign, George W. said he felt "burned out." He decided to go back into the oil business seriously. He started his own oil drilling busi-

George Bush for Congress

ON NOVEMBER 7,
VOTE FOR WEST TEXAS.
VOTE FOR
George Bush for Congress

Dear Voters,

Laura and I would like to take this opportunity to thank you for the many kindnesses you've shown us during my campaign for the Congress.

You've listened to me, and you've told me what you think. And hundreds of you have actively worked in my campaign.

I am very grateful to all of you.

During the past twelve months I have told you how much I want to represent you in the Congress. I mean that. I know I can do a good job.

Again, our thanks.

George W. Bush

A final plea for votes before the election.

ness. He called the company Arbusto, Spanish for "bush." Family friends helped him raise the money to start the company.

George W. was no absentee owner—he really ran the company. He was never a heavy-handed boss. "He hires good men and lets 'em do their job," says Jim McAninch, who had run the company's drilling operations. George W. knew what his strengths were. He didn't have a technical background. He was mainly a promoter and fundraiser. But he was also easy to get along with. People who worked with him liked him a lot. It seems that being an oil company executive is a lot like being a politician.

In fact, politics was never far from George W.'s life. He was always close to his father, and his father's political career was prospering. In addition to having been a congressman and chairman of the Republican National Committee, George Senior had also served as ambassador to the United Nations, chief of the U.S. liaison office in China, and Director of the Central Intelligence Agency (C.I.A.).

He made a lot of friends in the Republican party. So in 1980, he decided to try to get the Republican nomination for president. His chief rival was a former actor who had been governor of California, Ronald Reagan. Bush was an early favorite. Reagan was a better campaigner and won the nomination. After winning, Reagan sought to heal the split in his party by choosing George Bush as his running mate.

The Reagan/Bush team went on to win the 1980 election. They were reelected in 1984.

Back in Texas, George W.'s Arbusto company did well for a while. But the oil business is never steady. By 1982 the company was in financial trouble. He was helped out by a family friend.

When the oil business recovered in early 1983, all of the oil companies in Midland were making money—lots of it. A close friend of George W. says, "Those were the doodah days in Midland." A lot of people were spending their new wealth on things like fancy cars and personal jets. Not George W. His lifestyle didn't change. He had always been careful with money. Some people called him downright tight. Laura had to badger him to get a new suit or new shoes.

Perhaps because his family always had money, George W. Bush didn't seem to care very much about money. When you're running an oil company you have to care. And the oil business was just about to enter another bad time.

By late 1983 there were signs of real trouble again. The First National Bank of Midland collapsed. The bank had made a lot of loans to local oil companies, now the companies couldn't pay. Most of the oilmen figured that business would turn around in about a year. Their slogan became "Stay alive till '85." Oilmen are always hopeful. This time they were wrong. In 1985 business was even worse.

Laura, George W., the twins Barbara and Jenna, and Barbara Bush listen to George Sr. at a Reagan/Bush rally in Midland, Texas, 1984.

A portrait of the extended Bush family sitting in front of their home in Kennebunkport, Maine, in 1986.

George W. had run his business carefully. He could also depend on a network of wealthy investors. His company was not in as much trouble as many others. But it was in trouble. He took a 25 percent pay cut. His staff took smaller cuts. Nothing helped. The problems were way beyond his control.

In 1986 there was a real financial crash. The price of oil dropped from an already low $25 a barrel in January to $9 a barrel by spring. George W., who had been telling his employees, and himself, that hard times would last only a few more months, now knew that his company was going to last only a few more months.

Instead of going out of business, Bush sold his company to a larger company. Harken Oil & Gas, a big Texas-based company, stepped in with a sweet deal. Bush's investors got their money back. Many of his employees got jobs with Harken. George W. used his contacts to get jobs for all the others. George himself became a director and consultant for Harken. He was making more money than he ever had in his own company.

What was Harken getting for its money? The son of the vice president of the United States, that's what. "His name was George Bush. That was worth the money they paid him," said the founder of Harken.

In 1986 George W. Bush turned forty. It was to be a turning point in his life. He decided he had to make changes in the way he lived. One of the changes was in his drinking.

George W. gives the thumbs-up sign while on the road working on his father's presidential campaign.

As a fraternity boy in college he drank a lot at parties. As a Texas oilman he still drank a lot. "I didn't drink every minute of the day," he has said, "but I drank too much." For years Laura had urged him to stop drinking. Shortly after his fortieth birthday, he did.

George W. has said that he began to think about turning his life around after a meeting with the Reverend Billy Graham at the Bush family summer home in Maine in 1985. Graham, he said, "planted a seed in my heart and I began to change."

Some of his friends believe he had an additional reason for giving up drinking. His father was preparing to run for president. George W. didn't want to do anything that might be an embarrassment.

Being a director and consultant for Harken Oil and Gas didn't take a lot of George W.'s time. He had plenty of money, but he didn't have a real job. And he didn't have any clear plan about what he was going to do next.

He decided to take another look at politics.

Back in April 1985 Vice President Bush had called his family together at the presidential retreat at Camp David, Maryland. He told them that he was going to run for president when Ronald Reagan's second term ended.

He also introduced them to Lee Atwater, the man he had hired to run his campaign. Atwater was known as a brilliant but ruthless political strategist. He was also a political "hired gun," not a long-time family associate. Atwater had worked for other candidates. George W. wondered out loud whether he could be trusted. Atwater challenged him to come back and watch what he was doing. If he was being disloyal, then George W. could do something about it.

After the oil company collapse and buyout of 1986 George W. recalled the challenge. He and Laura sold their house in Midland, Texas, loaded up the family wagon, and drove east to Washington, D.C. Here he joined his father's presidential campaign.

At this point, George W. insists he had no plans to run for office again. In fact, his younger brother Jeb, a Florida real-estate developer, was considered the most promising politician among the Bush boys.

Political campaigns are very hard work. Members of a campaign staff spend long hours together and are always under pressure. Campaign staffs often split up into factions, groups that have different ideas about what is most important. George Bush's campaign staff was like that. It was split between Bush's vice presidential staff, and his hired campaign staff under Atwater. George W. or Junior, as he was usually called at that time, joined the Atwater faction.

George W. thought Atwater was doing a good job. He learned a lot from him. Atwater used Junior to influence George Senior, who was sometimes uncomfortable with Atwater's aggressive political tactics.

What had begun as an uneasy alliance soon grew into a real friendship. When Atwater was stricken with fatal brain cancer in 1990, George W. visited him regularly during his last days. He read the Bible at his dying friend's bedside.

Around the campaign office, Junior got the reputation of being something of a tough guy, an "enforcer."

A gathering in the Oval Office, December, 1989. From left to right are Andy Card, Assistant to the President, George W., John Sununu, Chief of Staff, Lee Atwater, Chairman of the Republican National Committee and President George Bush.

He made sure that the staff remained loyal and did their jobs properly. He was also known as a fellow who had a temper and was not afraid to lose it. He got into yelling matches with other staff members. He was nervous, energetic, impatient, and loud, in contrast to his lower-key brother, Jeb.

Bush Senior was impressed by the way his eldest son handled the campaign job. After George Bush was elected president, a lot of people assumed that Junior would stay in Washington. As the son of the president he would have a good deal of power and influence. So people were very surprised that after his father's inauguration, George W. again packed up his family and moved back to Texas. This time he went to Dallas. His friends thought he was planning to run for governor of Texas in an election that would be coming up in two years. But if that was his plan he didn't say anything in public.

George W. had a good shot at being elected governor. Since the days of President Lyndon Johnson, Texas had become an increasingly Republican state. George W. Bush was a Republican. He had campaigned for his father and other Republicans all over the state. He knew every important Republican in Texas.

Everybody in Texas certainly knew who George W. Bush was. He was the son of President George Bush. But that wasn't enough.

George W. has said, "My biggest problem in Texas is the question 'What's the boy ever done? He could be riding on his Daddy's name.'"

All he could really point to was the time he had spent working in his father's campaign and his years as head of a not very successful oil company. That wasn't enough.

When George W. got back to Texas after his father's election, he didn't have a job. But he had a pretty good idea of what he was going to do. Even before the presidential election he had been called by a former business partner who was putting together a group to buy the Texas Rangers baseball team that played in a Dallas suburb.

George W. had always been a great baseball fan. So was his father. Growing up near Houston, he had been a fan of the Houston Astros. The Astros, however, weren't for sale. The Rangers were.

The man selling the Rangers was an old Bush family friend, Eddie Chiles. Still, Chiles wasn't giving the team away. The asking price was well over $80 million.

George W. didn't have that kind of money. What he had was a large circle of wealthy and influential friends. He was able to put together a group that raised the money to buy the team. Bush himself put in a little over half a million.

George W. became one of two managing general partners. A title like "managing general partner" is a very loose one. Some of his political opponents have claimed that George W. was just a public relations front man. After all, he was the president's son, and he was bound to be noticed.

His friends say George W. was vital to the success of the team. And the team did succeed. Before George W. and his partners took it over the Rangers were a second-string team that was losing money. They were playing in an unattractive and unpopular converted minor league field. With a larger, fancier stadium, the club could make enough money to attract first-rate players.

The first order of business for the new owners of the Texas Rangers was to get a new and modern ballpark. Bush and his partners led a successful drive to build an impressive and attractive new stadium in Arlington, Texas.

George W. traveled around the state making speeches promoting his team. He attended every home game. He was right there behind the dugout. Everybody in the park could see him. So could everyone who watched the game on TV.

Here was the president's son. He owned the team. Yet he was out there eating hot dogs and drinking soda, just like any other fan. People would come up to shake his hand or ask for his autograph. George W. would always oblige. Sometimes he would stay in the park for an hour after the game signing autographs and talking to fans.

While promoting the Texas Rangers, George W. was also promoting himself. The people of Texas already knew his name because of his father. Now they were beginning to known him personally, for himself.

George W. had never been a very good public speaker. As he traveled around talking about baseball he sharpened his speaking skills.

He also sharpened his image as a good family man, and a decent, ordinary guy—not just some rich man's son from the East. His wife, Laura, often joined him at the ballpark. Though he had now become quite a rich

As the most visible part-owner of the Texas Rangers, George W. had his own fans who wanted his autograph.

George W. points out some of the special features of the new ballpark to reporters.

man in his own right, the Bush family still lived in a modest house. He avoided limos—his own or anybody else's—and drove his own car. And, as always, he was a very casual dresser.

In 1992, when President George Bush ran for reelection, George W. crisscrossed the state campaigning for his father. He had now developed a smooth approach that mixed politics, family values, and baseball.

President Bush carried Texas, but lost the national election to Bill Clinton. It was a bitter blow for the Bush family. President Bush had spent many years in federal government service. During his term as president, he had fought and won the Gulf War against Saddam Hussein of Iraq. After the Gulf War was over in 1990, President Bush's popularity was extremely high. Yet just two years later a governor from a small state defeated him.

In a way President Bush's defeat freed his two sons to go into politics. As long as their father held national office, they could never be really independent. Now with George Bush Senior out of politics, George W. and Jeb could actively pursue their own political careers—and they did.

Both ran for governor in 1994, George W. in Texas and Jeb in Florida. Jeb Bush lost narrowly to the very popular Democratic governor of Florida. George W. beat Ann Richards of Texas, another popular Democratic governor.

Defeating Richards may have been particularly sweet for the Bush family. At the 1988 Democratic National Convention she ridiculed Bush Senior's inherited wealth and tendency to flub his speeches. "Poor

George," she said, "he can't help it—he was born with a silver foot in his mouth." Even though Bush Senior won that election, the now-famous line haunted him throughout the rest of his career.

George W. couldn't match Ann Richards as a speaker, but he was a personable and very likable campaigner. George Bush Senior always seemed uncomfortable as a campaigner. George W. loved it. He would plunge into crowds, patting backs and grabbing hands and elbows in a Texan handshake. He liked getting up close to people.

George W. also controlled his temper and remained polite. He ignored Richards's jibes—she often called him "Shrub," a not very polite reference to his last name. He always called her governor. He kept to a few main campaign themes: improving education, reforming welfare, and making changes in the court system. He was folksy, friendly, and optimistic.

George W. now had a big accomplishment on his record. While the election campaign was just getting started, work on the new Texas Rangers stadium in Arlington was just being finished. The stadium opened in April 1994, seven months before the election. It was a project that George W. was closely identified with. It was something he could point to with pride. And he did.

Bush won with 53.5 percent of the vote.

George W. Bush threw himself into the job of being governor with all his characteristic energy. The governor

When George W. was campaigning with his father in 1992, his nephew joined them to visit Oriole Park in Baltimore, Maryland, to throw the opening pitch.

On January 17, 1994, with his wife, Laura, looking on, George W. Bush is sworn in as the new Governor of Texas.

of Texas does not have a great deal of independent power. In order to be successful, the governor has to work closely with the powerful Texas legislature. "The Ledge," as it is sometimes called, tends to go its own way.

George W. was able to work successfully with members of the legislature, both Republicans and Democrats. The accomplishments he is most proud of are improving the education system, reducing crime, and cutting taxes.

Like the governor of practically every other state in the late 1990s, Governor George W. Bush was lucky. His state benefited from nationwide prosperity. He also benefited from a nationwide drop in the crime rate. Like every other politician, Governor Bush was quick to claim credit for the good times.

Whatever Governor Bush was doing in Texas, people liked him for it. His popularity soared.

When 1998 rolled around, no one in Texas seriously doubted that the extremely popular and personable governor was going to be reelected. Very few predicted that he was suddenly going to become the odds-on favorite to win the Republican nomination for president, and perhaps the presidency itself.

Of course, he had been mentioned as a possible presidential candidate. He was just one of many possible Republican candidates.

At the start of 1998, President Clinton became enmeshed in scandal. For a while it looked as if he was going to have to resign. If he didn't he might be impeached and removed from office.

The Republicans also assumed that the Clinton scandal would drag down many congressional Democrats in the 1998 election. None of that happened. President Clinton was not removed from office. In the election, the Democrats actually gained seats in the House of Representatives. Polls showed that while the U.S. public did not like the way the president had behaved, they liked the way congressional Republicans had behaved even less.

On the other hand, Republican governors had done very well. This time Jeb Bush was elected in Florida. And George W. didn't just win reelection; he was absolutely swept back into office with 68.6 percent of the vote. He was the first Texas governor to be elected to consecutive four-year terms.

George W. Bush's big win in Texas made him a national figure. He had a well-known name. He was attractive and likable. He showed he could work with both the Republicans and the Democrats. He was, in short, the kind of man who might be elected president.

George W. made it clear that he wanted to be president. When he did the backers began lining up. The Bush family had a lot of friends. By the summer of 1999, George W. had raised more money than any other presidential candidate in history.

He looked like an easy choice for the Republicans. But there were rumors about his "wild youth." He

Sharing a laugh are, from left to right, George W., Governor of Texas, George Sr., former president of the United States, and Jeb, Governor of Florida.

responded, "When I was young and irresponsible, I was young and irresponsible." But he refused to answer questions about what he may have done twenty or more years ago.

During the primaries George W. received a surprisingly strong challenge from Arizona senator John McCain. McCain had been a prisoner of war in Vietnam, and was a genuine war hero. He was also a Republican, but was sometimes more popular with Independent voters and even some Democrats than he was with the core members of his own party. People faithful to the Republican Party rallied to Bush, who won most of the primaries. When the Republican convention opened in Philadelphia in the summer of 2000 there was no doubt that George W. Bush would be the nominee.

In choosing his vice presidential running mate, George W. looked to his family's inner circle and picked Dick Cheney. Cheney had been a congressman and secretary of defense during George Sr.'s presidency. He was known to be extremely smart, but as a candidate he had drawbacks. He was a stiff and uncomfortable campaigner. He didn't have a large personal following so there was no block of voters he could deliver. And he had already suffered several heart attacks. Voters might be worried about his health. But for George W., Dick Cheney had one quality that overshadowed all the negatives. He was a trusted Bush family friend.

The Democratic nominee was Al Gore, Bill Clinton's vice president. His running mate was Connecticut senator Joseph Lieberman.

The 2000 presidential election campaign was hard fought, but not bitter. Both candidates were moderates—with Republican Bush slightly to the right and Democrat Gore slightly to the left of center. There were differences, but times were good and the country was

*President-elect George W. Bush stands
with Vice-President-elect Dick Cheney, right,
and General Colin Powell, left, after nominating
Powell for secretary of state.*

not split by any deeply emotional issue like the civil rights struggle or the war in Vietnam.

Before the election the polls indicated that the race would be close. But they didn't say how close.

As the results came in on election night it first appeared as if Gore would be the winner. Then it looked like Bush was ahead. By morning the only thing that was certain was that the election was too close to call.

Al Gore had won the popular vote, narrowly but undeniably. He was also ahead in the all-important electoral vote. But there was one important state still undecided—Florida. Whichever candidate took that state and its 25 electoral votes would become president. This was by far the closest election the country had seen in over a hundred years.

Just to add to the drama, Florida's governor was Jeb Bush, George W.'s younger brother.

Bush held a lead of a few hundred votes out of over six million cast in the state. Some Florida voters and the Gore campaign contested the Florida vote on a variety of legal fronts, and the uncertainty dragged on for weeks. Many serious questions were raised about how we elect our presidents.

Then Dick Cheney had another heart attack. He was back on the job just a few days after getting out of the hospital, but all the old questions about his health resurfaced.

Finally, George W. Bush was declared the winner and Al Gore conceded. But the task that the newly elected president faces is a tough one.

More people had actually voted for his rival. The partisan bitterness that had not been part of the campaign had erupted in the postelection controversy. Many Democrats believed that Gore had really won the election. They regarded George W. Bush as an accidental president at best, an illegitimate president at worst.

The congressional elections showed a country split down the middle. The Senate is split 50 to 50. In the House of Representatives the Republicans cling to a tiny and reduced majority.

There are other clouds on the horizon. The economy, which for years had been amazingly strong, seemed to have taken a sharp downturn as the year 2000 ended. And in other parts of the world potential trouble spots, like the Middle East, were heating up again.

Throughout his campaign George W. Bush had described himself as a "unifier," the sort of person who could work with people who disagreed and bring them together.

There can be no doubt that this skill will be tested in the first years of George W. Bush's presidency.

Chronology

1946	Born July 6 in New Haven, Connecticut.
1948	Bush family moves to Texas.
1953	Sister Robin dies.
1961	Leaves Texas to enter Phillips Academy in Massachusetts.
1964	Enters Yale University.
1968	Joins Texas Air National Guard.
1973	Enters Harvard Business School.
1975	Begins work in oil and gas business in Midland, Texas.
1977	Marries Laura Welch. Runs unsuccessfully for Congress.
1981	Twin daughters Barbara and Jenna born.
1986	Sells interest in oil company.
1987	Joins father's campaign for president.
1989	Assembles group that buys Texas Rangers baseball franchise; becomes Managing General Partner.
1994	Elected Governor of Texas.
1998	Reelected governor in landslide.
1999	Becomes candidate for Republican presidential nomination.
2000	Elected President of the United States

Index